Lovers' Wisdom

Lovers' Wisdom

Judy Ashberg

PIATKUS

First published in 2004 by
Piatkus Books Ltd
5 Windmill Street
London W1T 2JA
email: info@piatkus.co.uk
website: www.piatkus.co.uk
author website: www.uniquewisdom.co.uk

The moral right of the author has been asserted

A catalogue record for this book is available
from the British Library

ISBN 0 7499 2568 X

Text design by Briony Chappell

This book has been printed on paper manufactured
with respect for the environment using wood from
managed sustainable resources.

Printed and bound in Great Britain by
CPI Bath

For C,
without whom this book could
never have been written.

contents

finding
love

The best way to have a happy
relationship is to work on your
own self-esteem.

When you feel good about
yourself, you will attract the right
people into your life and you will
not tolerate a partner who does
not treat you in the way
you would like.

Do you find yourself constantly making bad choices in relationships? Think about why you are drawn to people who are not right for you. If you can learn more about yourself and your own needs and desires, you will have a much greater chance of happiness in future relationships.

Just because you have failed
at one or even a few serious
relationships, it doesn't mean
you may not succeed in finding the
right person eventually. You can
learn from past mistakes.

Some people look for one perfect partner and never find him or her. By recognising your own imperfections, you will be more likely to tolerate and accept flaws in others.

If you are taking a while to meet the right person, keep your heart open. If you become attached to a negative way of thinking, you will push people away, or worse, you might not recognise the right person when they do show up.

Be aware of repeating patterns!
If you grew up in a single-parent
household, or if one of your parents
was often away, you may find
yourself attracted to a partner
who is also often absent.

It can be hard to have a happy relationship with a partner if your parents didn't enjoy one while you were growing up. As an adult, try to model your relationship on one you know is happy, tolerant and respectful.

When we first fall in love,
we usually see only good qualities
in our partner. Over the years,
we will also get to know the
darker side of their character.
Successful relationships happen
when partners commit for
better or worse.

Beware of critical people.
No one wants their lover to put
them down, either privately
or in public.

Beware of jealous and possessive people too. They are very difficult to live with. Think carefully if your new lover seems to want to separate you from family and friends who love you and have your best interests at heart.

Many people are afraid to enter into a long-lasting commitment because they have seen so many unhappy relationships. But many relationships are wonderfully happy. If you have chosen your partner wisely and with care, there is no reason why you should not live happily ever after.

A close and intimate relationship
exposes all our vulnerabilities.
Be sure you feel emotionally safe
with a person before you commit to
sharing your life with them.

Be the best person you can be
with your lover and give them
whatever you are able to give.
With the right person, there is no
need to hold back. Both of you
deserve the best of each other.

Making a commitment can be like
diving off a cliff into the sea –
scary but exhilarating.
Both require courage, but the
rewards will be worth it.

When we fall in love, we offer the gift of unconditional love to each other. This is what makes this time in our lives so special.

When we are in love, we are likely to be at our least clear-headed and detached at a time when we should be at our most careful and objective. So always take your time before making important decisions.

Everyone deserves to have good relationships. Never feel guilty because you are in a good relationship and other people are not. None of us knows what the future may bring.

Your partner might seem perfect when you first fall in love, but as you get to know each other, you will learn that no one is perfect. Not even you.

When you meet a person you love and want to live with, constantly affirm to yourself that you deserve to have a wonderful relationship. If you convince yourself that your relationships are never going to work out, they won't!

If things are not working out in your relationship, take a long hard look at yourself. You may be with the wrong partner.

Every relationship is different.
There are no rules on how you
should experience them.

Sometimes we worry too much about what people outside our relationship might think about our partner. We need be concerned only with what is right for us and not what others may or may not be thinking.

We have to make difficult choices in our relationships. We often need to give ourselves time to know what we are and are not prepared to settle for.

Honesty is not always the best policy. It pays to be tactful.

Sometimes our parents and our friends can tell if our partner is the right one for us; sometimes they can't. Pay attention to their views but in the end you have to make the final choice.

If you feel that 'any man' or 'any woman' is better than no one at all, you are very unlikely to end up with the right person.

If you are a loving person but you grew up in a household where you were criticised, you may in turn become critical of others.
Be aware of this in yourself so that it doesn't cause problems in your relationship.

Talk, talk, talk. Talk as much as you can with your partner about all your hopes and dreams for the future. If you have very different views and values on important aspects of life, such as money or where to live, think about what will happen if your partner does not ever change his or her views.

Money is an emotive issue. Think about your views on money very carefully before you start living together. The higher-earner is often – though not always – the person who has the most power in the relationship.

Women who want to be married should take care before moving in with lovers who have not proposed. Once you are living together – and your lover is receiving all the benefits of marriage – there is no longer any incentive for him to make the kind of commitment you want.

Don't contribute to your lover's mortgage without considering whether to draw up a legal agreement between you. This will ensure that you receive your fair share of the property if you decide to separate.

If your partner is causing you to feel unhappy before you move in with each other, they are unlikely to make you feel any happier when you are living together.

Before you move in together, talk about your feelings and attitudes towards fidelity. This is not a subject to take for granted.

Your wedding day can involve months of exciting planning. But what about after the wedding? Your relationship can seem like a complete anti-climax with little to look forward to. Make plans for the weeks and years ahead, so your wedding will be just a part of the wonderful store of memories you will be building during your life together.

Weddings are emotional and intense events for everyone involved. Always allow for this when you are making your plans to ensure that you can differentiate between your own emotions and the strong feelings of others.

*Do not be seduced by dreams of
your wedding day and find yourself
married to the wrong person.*

Do not settle down with the wrong person just to give your children a parent.

Not everyone wants to be a parent. A person who does not want children may not be persuaded to change their mind. Talk this through carefully before you decide to build a life together.

Everyone is unique and everyone has their own inner wisdom. Give yourself the time and space to listen to what your heart is really telling you and you will always make the right choices.

'When you are in love with the
right person, life is truly glorious.

*making
love*

Good sex is wonderful at any time.
There is no such thing as 'normal'.
Every couple is unique.

The more intimate, honest and open your relationship is, the more it will affect your sex life in a positive way.

*Accept that not every partner
will be romantic or creative enough
to fulfil all your fantasies.
Sometimes you have to spell out
in detail what it is you really
want and tell each other what
turns you on – and off.*

Physical intimacy is very important in a long-term relationship. Be aware that if your partner has very different sexual needs from you this could cause problems in the future.

Everyone likes to be told that their partner had a good time.

Surprise each other with new ideas for making love together. Never get complacent – you'll miss out on so much pleasure!

If you and your lover are
frequently too tired to make love
at the end of the day, try
scheduling dates in your diary to
spend a lazy evening together
– in bed, making love.

Living without sex can create many problems in a relationship. Do your best to be open and honest with each other and talk through the situation together as best you can. You may need to seek professional help.

Great sex is wonderful, and
you can't have too much of it.
If you love each other, always
make an effort, especially as
you grow older.

People's bodies always tell the truth – especially in bed. Your body can tell you what is going on in your relationship before your mind has realised it.

Making love is great fun, romantic and exciting. It's even good for your health. When times get tough, good sex can remind you of why you were attracted to one another – and why you want to keep the relationship alive.

When sex works, it is truly glorious. So always persevere in finding what suits you both.

It can take many months – and sometimes years – for couples to achieve their best ever sexual experiences. There is always a new approach to explore if you get bored.

It's amazing how your sex life
will improve if you tackle the
household chores together.

It takes courage and honesty to be vulnerable and surrender, and your relationship will surely be rewarded by it.

Great sex is risky, but it can lead to the best physical experiences that life has to offer.

The best sex is about
communicating with each other
in the deepest and most
profound way.

family and
friends

Whatever your background, the way your parents lived and experienced their relationship will affect how you relate to your partner. You will be surprised by how much you recreate your childhood experiences in your mature relationships.

Observe how closely the pattern of your relationship mirrors that of your parents. Be aware of the things that you disliked in your parents' relationships and make sure that you do not find yourself repeating them with your partner.

We often choose a partner who behaves like our parents. If we get angry with our partners, we need to recognise that it may be our relationship with our parents that needs attention – not our relationship with our partner.

We grow up with certain patterns in our early family relationships and we often unconsciously fall in love with people whose characters are similar to one or other of our parents. So when we meet these people, it can feel wonderfully and delightfully familiar to be with them.

If you find it hard to communicate with your partner in the way that you want to, think about how you communicated in the family you grew up in. What was the pattern you learned in the past? When you can recognise it, you'll find it easier to change how you behave with the person you love.

If you want your partnership to succeed, you must put your relationship first. Do not let your families come between you and your partner, however much you love them and however much they love you.

Views about money are frequently shaped by the family you grew up in. But your financial upbringing and values may be very different from those of your partner. You need to look at the different ways in which your two families manage their money and recognise why you may be arguing about it.

Many couples are constantly stressed by the competing demands of work, home and family. We need to find frequent ways of switching off so that we can concentrate more on each other and enjoy good times together.

If you find you are confiding your innermost thoughts to friends or family instead of to your partner, take a long look at what is going on in your relationship. Why are you denying your partner the most intimate part of you – probably the part that he or she fell in love with?

Some families argue constantly with one another because that is the only way they know to feel connected. Is your family background like that? If it is, and you and your partner are bickering, you may simply be recreating what you are used to.

Develop your own unique relationship rituals and family traditions which have meaning for you and your partner.

Everyone needs support from family and friends. We cannot expect our partner to fulfil all our emotional needs, but be careful that external support does not come between you and your partner.

If you find your in-laws or your partner's children difficult to deal with, do your best to remain calm and detached. Where possible let your partner resolve problematic issues directly with his or her parent and children.

When your partner and your parents do not get on, you have to acknowledge that you cannot change their views about each other. All you can do is encourage everyone to respect one another's differences and choose to spend time with your parents on your own.

'Bringing up children, however much you love them, can feel very onerous at times. It is important for your relationship that you take some time out together as a couple and enjoy yourselves!

Children are very sensitive to the subtle nuances in their parents' relationships. If your child suddenly begins to behave badly, look first at what is going on between you and your partner — or what other issues may be happening in your lives together.

Do not allow your child to become a substitute for your partner in your affections. Your relationship as a family will be more successful when your relationship as adults and lovers comes first.

Children can be manipulative. Always do your best to present a united front to your children so that they are unable to play one of you off against the other. This will make them feel safe and secure when they are growing up and will also ensure there is less conflict between you.

There is no such thing as perfection in parenting as each child will follow their own path in life. Trust that you are doing the best that you can in today's competitive society and praise each other for the many things you get right. All children are happier when they live with happy parents.

being together

Happiness is waking up every morning and knowing that the person lying beside you is the one you want to be with. Being able to spend your adult years living with the right partner is the greatest gift you can have.

Always hang on to your sense of humour. A relationship without humour and laughter is never happy. Share all the laughs and happy moments that you can.

Say loving and kind things to each other as often as you can. It sounds so simple when you are first in love but keeping it up over time will pay dividends throughout your life.

Be thoughtful and considerate of each other. If you get in the habit of doing this early in your relationship, it becomes much easier to keep it up every day.

Try not to take anything for granted. Compliment and thank your partner for all that they do for you. When people say loving things to one another, both feel cherished and cared for.

In a loving and happy relationship, good communication is everything. Try to recognise when you are getting out of the habit of communicating and take gradual steps to start again.

We must recognise that what we want is not necessarily what our partner wants. Try to ask for what you need and explain what is not right for you.

Some people are brought up in homes where they are not allowed to express their anger. Many relationships founder because one partner does not know how to express their anger in a mature and acceptable way. It is important to learn how to do this.

Some people find it difficult to say 'no'. Learning to say 'no' pleasantly but firmly is essential and empowering. If you cannot stand up for yourself you can become full of resentment.

Always treat your partner the way you would like to be treated.

Some couples consider present-giving to be very important. If your partner is not very good at finding you the perfect gift, simply tell them what you would like and ask them to buy it for you. This is the easy way to avoid disappointment.

If your partner is bad at remembering birthdays and anniversaries, don't suffer in silence. Simply remind them about the date and tell them what you would like to do. Planning an event together – or even by yourself – is an enjoyable way to know that you will have the celebration you would really like.

Do not live your life through your partner. Stick up for your own opinions, ideas, emotions, relationships and everything that contributes to making you the fabulous person who they fell in love with. Learn to separate what is yours from what is theirs.

Always make space for time to be
on your own. No one wants to
feel smothered in their relationship
so you need to separate and come
together again in ways that
suit you both.

Touch, kiss, and hold each other close. All of these are daily reminders of how much you care for each other. Even when you are angry, a light touch from one to another can soothe and heal.

Sometimes, you may simply want and need to be held and loved. Your partner may not realise this so you have to ask for it.

'Your partner is not a mind-reader
so get used to saying how you feel.

True listening is hearing what is unspoken. Really listen to each other and do your best to understand what your partner is trying to tell you. Don't just wait for your turn to speak.

When the outside world is tough, you need to know that the person you come home to is on your side.

One way to check whether you are in a good relationship is to ask yourself how it really feels. A good relationship feels good and solid – even when the two people are angry with one another.

When your partner does apologise for a trivial mistake or wrongdoing, accept their apology graciously and don't continue to give them a hard time.

'We are often attracted to people who are different from us emotionally. Once we can accept difference in our emotional outlook – and can respect it – there will be less to argue about.

It is not our differences we need to be concerned about. It is how we work together to resolve them.

Are you a nag?
Nothing destroys the fabric of an
otherwise loving relationship more
than constant nagging.

A small and kindly act can settle
an impasse and help you progress
towards something better.

If your partner is unable to stay faithful, only you can decide whether or not to settle for this.

Childish tantrums have no place in a mature adult relationship.

You do not need to persuade
your partner to think like you do.
You simply have to agree to differ.
Let go of having to be right.
Neither of you needs to be
right or wrong.

Try not to be bitter. Bitterness
destroys everything in your life
and will prevent you ever
being happy.

Obstinacy is very difficult to handle in a relationship. Ask yourself why you are so committed to this particular way of thinking. What will happen if you dare to become more flexible?

Do you get irritated with your partner? Large amounts of patience and understanding are required at these times. This is one of the secrets of successful relationships.

Think before you speak.
You can think it but maybe you
don't need to say it.

You may be living with a lovely partner but not feeling happy. Do not expect your partner to be able to solve your emotional problems for you. Learn more about yourself and why you are the way you are, so that you understand what you need to do to find happiness.

If you have had a stressful day, make time to share your troubles with your partner instead of taking your bad mood out on them. If you have both had a bad day, try to think of something funny which happened in the day that you can both have a laugh about.

Sometimes we expect too much from life. We do not always recognise how lucky we already are.

*through
thick and
thin*

Put aside thoughts of 'winning' or 'losing' when it comes to your partner. You have to think in terms of what is best for the relationship – which means both of you – if you want to be together in the years to come.

Harsh words spoken in anger can
never be taken back.

Love is about saying you are
sorry when you know you are
in the wrong.

We all want to be loved
unconditionally and accepted for
the person we truly are. We want
this to continue throughout our
lives together, however difficult it
may sometimes be.

All relationships go through difficult times because of external events. Each person will have their own way of coping. Some people require togetherness; others need to be on their own. Always respect your partner's differences from yours at these times.

There are periods in a long-term relationship when one partner is giving much more than the other. In a good relationship, this will even out over time.

A couple who can solve the problem of who does the ironing is set fair for a good life together.

Celebrate everything you can. Celebrate birthdays, anniversaries, promotions and every good fortune you can think of. Celebrating regularly reminds you both how many good things there are in your lives together.

Try not to become boring. Some people blame partners for leaving them when they themselves have nothing of interest to say. Do not rely on your partner to create all the conversation and excitement in your relationship. Develop a life of your own that you can share.

One of the great pleasures of a good relationship is making plans together. While you don't want to live in the past – or totally in the future – it is fun to share your memories and build your dreams for the years to come.

A good relationship is like a plant.
You have to look after it and
nurture it or it will wither and
die from neglect.

The qualities we found so attractive in our partner when we first fell in love, are often the things that exasperate us the most when we know each other better.

Sometimes we do not let our partners know how much we love them until it is too late. Then we cannot forgive ourselves. Make sure you tell your partner how you feel about them not just when you are angry but also when you are happy.

We should not overprotect our partners as one day they may need to function without us.

Arguments are often not about the issue that appears on the surface. If you can give yourself the opportunity to step back and ask yourself 'what is this argument really about?' you may be surprised by the answer.

People often argue more during times of great anxiety and concern. Recognise that these arguments can be a distraction to stop you thinking and talking about the fundamental thing that is worrying you.

Sometimes our relationships become stuck in a rut and we get bored. It may be much easier to try to climb out of the rut together than to consider separation because of it.

One person can change the dynamics of a relationship by altering their thoughts, attitudes and behaviour if they choose to.

Blaming your partner when things aren't working out is not productive. Work on your own self-esteem. People with good self-esteem rarely blame others for anything.

Everyone wants to be told they look good, however old they are and however long they have been in a relationship. Taking the time to look good for your partner (as well as for yourself) should continue for all the years you are together. Always acknowledge it.

No relationship is problem-free.
What makes one more successful
than another is the way in which
we overcome our differences and
resolve our conflicts.

When you are upset with your partner try to explain how you feel by focusing on their behaviour and not on them as people. Try to separate the person you love from what they actually did. This approach will be less corrosive.

When you fight, try to fight fair. However angry you are, avoid constantly bringing up past hurts. It will not help you resolve the current conflict and it will make it much harder for your partner to feel emotionally safe with you in the future.

Some people are good at bearing
a grudge. But bearing a grudge
simply stops you having as much
love in your life as you want
and need.

In love, or out of love, there are no right or wrong answers.

Living together, year after year, with the person you love gives you the opportunity to be the best person you can be.

Try to do things together which take you out of the home. Just going for a walk – or changing your regular routine – can refresh and restore your relationship.

You may share a life but you do not have to share everything you own. Each person needs to have their own space and their own possessions.

Be tolerant of each other's foibles. And, in turn, expect your partner to be tolerant of yours. Love each other in spite of everything.

For many people we are living in a Golden Age. We have our basic needs fulfilled – food, shelter, friends and family and a choice of meaningful work. We must remember how much more we have than any generations before us, on the days we fall prey to wishing we had even more.

Every relationship goes through hard times. No one escapes the fate that life has in store for them. Try to count your blessings as much and as often as you can.

Be proud of yourself and of each other. Be proud of your achievements individually and as a couple. Know you have always done the best you could.

Relationships are hard work.
But with the right person by your
side, the rewards are the best of
what life has to offer.

As you live happily over the years and build a wonderful life together, you will have the opportunity to experience greater and greater joy and happiness.

Also by Judy Ashberg:
LITTLE BOOK OF
WOMEN'S WISDOM

For information about
Judy Ashberg and to find
more thought-provoking insights
and inspiration:
www.uniquewisdom.co.uk